MOLLY'S PILGRIM AND
MAKE A WISH, MOLLY

by
Barbara Cohen

Teacher Guide

Written by
Sammie Underwood

Flower Rd. & Jerusalem Ave.
N. Massapequa, N.Y. 11758

Note

The 2005 Harper Trophy paperback edition of *Molly's Pilgrim*, © 1983 by Barbara Cohen, and the 1995 Yearling paperback edition of *Make a Wish, Molly*, © 1994 by the estate of Barbara K. Cohen, were used to prepare this guide. The page references may differ in other editions. *Molly's Pilgrim* ISBN: 978-0-688-16280-1 *Make a Wish, Molly* ISBN: 0-440-41058-4

Please note: Please assess the appropriateness of these books for the age level and maturity of your students prior to reading and discussing the texts with them.

ISBN: 978-1-60539-006-2

To order, contact your local school supply store, or—

Novel Units, Inc.
P.O. Box 97
Bulverde, TX 78163-0097

Web site: www.novelunits.com

Copyright infringement is a violation of Federal Law.

© 2008 by Novel Units, Inc., Bulverde, Texas. All rights reserved. No part of this publication may be reproduced, translated, stored in a retrieval system, or transmitted in any way or by any means (electronic, mechanical, photocopying, recording, or otherwise) without prior written permission from ECS Learning Systems, Inc.

Photocopying of student worksheets by a classroom teacher at a non-profit school who has purchased this publication for his/her own class is permissible. Reproduction of any part of this publication for an entire school or for a school system, by for-profit institutions and tutoring centers, or for commercial sale is strictly prohibited.

Novel Units is a registered trademark of ECS Learning Systems, Inc.
Printed in the United States of America.

Schwarting School Library
Flower Rd. & Jerusalem Ave.
N. Massapequa, N.Y. 11758

Table of Contents

Skills and Strategies

Vocabulary
Context, definitions,
synonyms, parts of speech

Comprehension
Inferring, predicting,
brainstorming, drawing
conclusions, identifying
attributes, supporting
judgments

Critical Thinking
Research, cause/effect,
compare/contrast,
problem solving

Literary Elements
Characterization, conflict,
dialogue, genre, theme,
author's purpose

Writing
Letter, lyrics, creative writing

Listening and Speaking
Discussion, oral presentation

Across the Curriculum
Art—illustration, poster,
collage; Math—graph;
Social Studies—map skills,
Bill of Rights, cultural studies

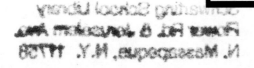

Genre: fiction

Setting: Winter Hill, Massachusetts; 1880s to 1920s

Point of View: first person

Themes: racism, pride, courage, peer pressure, fitting in, coming-of-age

Conflict: person vs. person, person vs. self, person vs. society

Style: narrative

Tone: innocent, confiding, honest

Dates of First Publication: *Molly's Pilgrim*—1983, *Make a Wish, Molly*—1994

Summary

Molly's Pilgrim: Molly and her family are Jewish immigrants from Russia who have moved to Winter Hill after living in New York City. Some children in Molly's third-grade class tease her because she is different. Through a school Thanksgiving activity, Molly and her classmates learn that the American Thanksgiving is modeled after the Jewish Feast of Tabernacles and that Molly and her family are Pilgrims, too.

Make a Wish, Molly: Molly attends a birthday party for the first time, and Elizabeth cruelly reveals Molly's unfamiliarity with American customs. Because she does not want anyone to know she and her family are different, Molly decides not to have a birthday party. When Emma, Fay, and Elizabeth surprise Molly at home on her birthday, Molly's mother hosts an "unplanned" party. Molly sees her mother in a new light and realizes that she and her family may not be that different after all.

About the Author

Barbara Cohen was born in New Jersey on March 15, 1932. When she was eight years old, her parents purchased the Somerville Inn, where she spent most of her childhood. Barbara and her family were of Jewish descent and grew up in an area where there was much prejudice against Jewish people. Since both her mother and father worked at the Inn during a time when mothers usually did not work, Barbara felt different and isolated from other children. For company, she turned to books.

Growing up, Barbara wrote often. She later attended college as an English major and then became a high-school English teacher. She married Gene Cohen and had three daughters, Leah, Sarah, and Becky, but did not write while raising her children. After a 20-year break from writing, Barbara published her first book, *The Carp in the Bathtub*, in 1972. Many of her stories are influenced by events she and her children experienced as Jews. "All of my writing is in some way inspired by my experience," Barbara once said, "but is only now and then a direct recounting of that experience." Barbara Cohen died on November 29, 1992, in Bridgewater, New Jersey.

Background Information

The Jewish culture dates back to the beginning of recorded history and exists all over the world. Historically, Jews have been exiled, imprisoned, beaten, and even killed because of their customs and beliefs. Others forbid them to practice their religion and force them to convert to Christianity. Jewish children were often not allowed to attend school.

In Russia, the rulers encouraged *pogroms*, raids on Jewish settlements in which homes and businesses were destroyed and people were beaten or killed. Most Jews were forced to relocate to an area of Russia called The Pale of Settlement. Many Jews responded to this discrimination by immigrating to America. Between 1882 and 1924, almost two million Jews fled to the United States for religious freedom and a better life.

The Jewish Feast of Tabernacles is called *Sukkot*, meaning booths or huts. This feast is similar to the American Thanksgiving holiday. On this holiday Jewish people give thanks to God for the earth's blessings and the crops produced that year. The celebration lasts for seven days and reminds the people of their ancestors who wandered in the wilderness for 40 years. The families build huts of branches or other natural materials and decorate them with fruits and vegetables as a reminder of their ancestors' temporary houses in the wilderness. During the worship service, Jewish people smell the *etrog*, a fruit resembling a lemon, and wave branches to the north, south, east, and west to show that God is everywhere.

Passover is one of the most important celebrations of the Jewish year. It lasts for seven days and seven nights in honor of the biblical story of God's freeing the Jews from centuries of slavery. Passover celebrations include a special meal of foods similar to those that the Jews ate on the night they escaped. The meal is served on a special plate called the Seder Plate. Two of the foods on the plate—a roasted egg and a roasted lamb bone—represent Jewish people's worship of God in the old Temple. These two items are not eaten. Jewish people eat pungent herbs such as horseradish to remind them of slavery's bitterness, greens such as parsley to represent the springtime, and an apple, nut, and wine mixture that symbolizes the mortar Jewish slaves used to make bricks. After the meal, the story of the Jews' escape from slavery is retold. During Passover, Jewish people abstain from eating anything that contains yeast or leavening in honor of their ancestors, who were forced to leave quickly and could not wait for their bread to rise. Instead, Jewish people eat a flat bread called *matzah*. Today, Passover is a time to celebrate freedom and hope for the future.

Characters

Molly: third-grade Jewish girl; immigrated from Russia with her family

Elizabeth: Molly's classmate; popular but mean girl; teacher's pet; teases Molly about being different

Emma: Molly's classmate; kind and thoughtful girl who befriends Molly

Miss Stickley: Molly's third-grade teacher

Mama: Molly's mother; doesn't speak English well; strong woman who loves her daughter

Papa: Molly's father; works at Mr. Brodsky's Variety Store

Fay: Molly's classmate; attends Molly's "unplanned party" and befriends Molly

Mrs. DeWitt: Emma's mother

Initiating Activities

1. Prereading: Prior to introducing the book, read aloud several books or stories that tell the Thanksgiving story. Be sure that students understand who the Pilgrims were, when and why they came to America, where they came from, and the hardships they faced. As you read, write details that students need to remember on sentence strips. Have students choose one sentence strip to illustrate. Display the sentence strips and illustrations in the classroom.

2. Research: Make a large KWL chart (see p. 15 of this guide) on posterboard. List things that students "know" about Judaism and/or Jewish culture in the "K" section. List questions that students have about these topics in the "W" section. Have students research the questions. Record their answers in the "L" section, and display the chart in the classroom. (Note: Be sure to include the persecution of Jews, particularly Russian Jews, in your discussion. This topic is significant to both novels.)

3. Social Studies: Give each student a copy of the Bill of Rights, and ask students to list examples of each freedom it guarantees. Hold a discussion about the Bill of Rights and its importance to our freedom.

4. Prereading: As you introduce the novels, instruct students to complete the Getting the "Lay of the Land" activity on page 16 of this guide.

Vocabulary Activities

1. Sentence Strips: Write each vocabulary word on a sentence strip, and assign each word to a different student. Have the student define the word and use it in a sentence on another sentence strip. Post the students' sentence strips in the classroom for students to access while reading.

2. Secret Word: Provide students a list of all vocabulary words. Select a "secret word," and read aloud clues that will help students determine the secret word (e.g., "The secret word is not a verb," "The secret word does not contain the letter 'S,'" "The secret word means _____," etc.). Students will eliminate vocabulary words until only one is left. Play as a whole group to demonstrate how the game is played, and divide the class into small groups for continued play.

3. Vocabulary Drawing: Have each student choose three vocabulary words and write them on a slip of paper. Place the slips in a hat or container, and have each student draw a slip. Students should write three sentences in which they correctly use the vocabulary words on the slip they have drawn. Have the students share their sentences in small groups to complete the activity.

4. Vocabulary Quiz: Provide students a list of all vocabulary words. Randomly recite definitions of 15 vocabulary words to the class. Have students write the correct vocabulary word for each definition on a sheet of paper.

Molly's Pilgrim: Section One, pp. 1–11

Molly and her parents live in Winter Hill. They moved to America from Russia, where they were persecuted for being Jewish. In school, Molly's classmates tease her because she is different. Molly hates school and wants to return to New York City or Russia, even though she knows this isn't possible.

Vocabulary
admired
peppermint
cushion
Yiddish
Jewish
tenement
Goraduk
Cossacks
synagogue
ignorant
interrupted

Discussion Questions

1. Why doesn't Molly enjoy school? *(She feels different because there are no other Jewish children. The kids tease and laugh at her.)*

2. Describe Elizabeth. *(Elizabeth is popular, conceited, and mean. She laughs at and insults Molly at every opportunity and sings a song that makes fun of Molly. At recess, she gives peppermint sticks to Molly's classmates but never to Molly.)*

3. Where did Molly live before she and her family moved to Winter Hill? *(New York City and Goraduk, Russia)*

4. List two reasons why Molly's family cannot move back to New York City and two reasons they cannot move back to Goraduk. Do you think Molly and her family should stay in Winter Hill? Why or why not? *(Molly and her parents cannot return to New York because life was more difficult for them there. In New York, Papa worked in a factory and the family had to live in a tenement house. The family cannot move back to Russia because they would likely be subjects of violence and oppression. The Cossacks burned down a nearby synagogue and could threaten the safety of Molly's family. Jewish girls in Russia cannot attend school, so Molly would not receive an education. Answers will vary. Suggestion: Most students will probably agree that Molly and her family should stay in Winter Hill, where Papa has a good job and the family lives in a nice apartment.)*

5. Why doesn't Molly want Miss Stickley or Elizabeth to see her mother? *(Molly's mother doesn't speak English well. She doesn't look like the other mothers.)*

6. **Prediction:** Will Molly's situation improve?

Supplementary Activities

1. Social Studies: Find a map of Russia during the early twentieth century and another map of present-day Russia. Compare the area that Russia covers on the first map to the second map. What conclusions can you draw from this information?

2. Characterization: Begin the Character Web for Molly on page 17 of this guide. Add to it as you read.

3. Music: Write a song about Molly that focuses on Molly's good qualities.

4. Writing: Use the newspaper graphic (see p. 18 of this guide) to write an article in which you describe at least one thing that is good about your school (e.g., a class you enjoy, a teacher you admire, a friend, the library, etc.). Be sure to include a headline in big letters at the top of the page.

Molly's Pilgrim: Section Two, pp. 12–28

Molly stammers over the word "Thanksgiving" while reading in school. Molly's mother makes a doll for Molly's Thanksgiving project. The doll looks like a Jewish immigrant instead of a traditional Pilgrim. Molly brings the doll to school, and Elizabeth and other students laugh. Miss Stickley explains to the class that Molly and her mother are Pilgrims, too.

Vocabulary
especially
corkscrew
celebrate
stumble
Pilgrims
cardboard
embroidered
kerchief
murmur
magnificent
headdress
hooted
harvest
Tabernacles
announced

Discussion Questions

1. How does Elizabeth respond when Molly says she does not know about Thanksgiving? What can you infer about Elizabeth's feelings toward Molly? *(Elizabeth says, "I thought everyone knew that…. I guess you people don't celebrate American holidays" [p. 12]. Answers will vary but should include that Elizabeth thinks Molly is stupid and un-American.)*

2. What does Miss Stickley say she is tired of doing every Thanksgiving? Why do you think she feels this way? What does Miss Stickley decide to do instead? *(Miss Stickley says she is tired of decorating the classroom with paper turkeys and pumpkins. Answers will vary but may include that paper decorations do not convey the true meaning or importance of Thanksgiving. Miss Stickley decides to have the class create a model of the Pilgrim village at Plymouth, Massachusetts, where the Pilgrims celebrated the first Thanksgiving.)*

3. How does Molly describe Pilgrims to her mother? *(Molly says that "Pilgrims came to this country from the other side…. They came for religious freedom. They came so they could worship God as they pleased" [p. 16].)*

4. Who does Mama's Pilgrim resemble? Why do you think Mama wants her doll to look this way? *(Mama's Pilgrim resembles Mama as a young Jewish girl. Answers will vary but should include that Mama sees herself as a Pilgrim. She and her family came to America for the same reasons as the Pilgrims.)*

5. From whom does Miss Stickley say that the Pilgrims got the idea for Thanksgiving? *(the Jewish feast of Tabernacles)*

6. Why does Miss Stickley put Molly's Pilgrim on her desk? *(to remind everyone that Pilgrims are still coming America)*

7. How is Emma different from Elizabeth? *(Emma does not hate Molly just because Molly is different. She thinks Molly's Pilgrim is the most beautiful of all.)*

Supplementary Activities

1. Art: Use the description on page 18 of the novel to draw a picture of Molly's Pilgrim. Color your illustration when you are finished drawing.

2. Compare/Contrast: Use the Venn diagram on page 19 of this guide to compare and contrast the Jewish Feast of Tabernacles and Thanksgiving.

Make a Wish, Molly: Section One, pp. 1–11

Molly begins to like school in the spring because she and Emma are friends. Emma invites Molly to her birthday party, and Molly learns that American birthday celebrations are much different from those in Russia. Molly is disappointed that she cannot sample Emma's birthday cake because the party takes place during Passover.

Vocabulary
permanent
position
butcher
curlicues
babka
strudel
rugelach
favor
Parcheesi
flourishes
seamstress
R.S.V.P.
maroon
leavening
matzo

Discussion Questions

1. Why doesn't Molly hate school as she did in the fall? *(She and Emma have become friends.)*

2. Describe Elizabeth's idea of a wonderful joke. Do you think Elizabeth's idea is funny? Why or why not? *(Elizabeth explains to Molly that everyone who attends Emma's party must bring a present. Then Elizabeth tells Molly, "I should never have told you. Then you'd have come without a present. You'd have felt silly. That would have been a wonderful joke" [p. 5]. Answers will vary. Suggestion: No, because it is not funny to hurt other people's feelings, nor is it fun to make people look silly.)*

3. Describe Molly's birthday present to Emma. Why do you think Mama chooses this gift? *(Molly gives Emma beautiful doll clothes: a summer dress made from white dotted swiss, a maroon velvet winter dress, and a plaid wool coat and hat. Answers will vary. Suggestion: Mama probably chooses this gift because she is a skilled seamstress. She knows she can make beautiful doll clothes that will not be too expensive.)*

4. Whom does Molly assume is coming to visit? *(Bubbe and Zayde, Molly's grandparents)*

5. What disappointing news does Molly learn? What is Molly's solution? How does Mama respond to Molly's solution? *(Molly learns that Emma's birthday party will take place during Passover. Jewish people can only eat certain foods during this time, and Molly is disappointed because she cannot sample Emma's birthday cake. Molly wants to forget about Passover for one afternoon. Mama objects to Molly's solution and reminds Molly that Passover is a time to be thankful. Because the family no longer lives in oppressive Russia, Mama says they should be especially thankful for their newfound freedom in America.)*

6. **Prediction:** Will Molly eat the cake at Emma's birthday party?

Supplementary Activities

1. Art/Social Studies: Create a poster to display at your own birthday party. Use pictures, drawings, magazine or newspaper clippings, etc., to show events, people, or things associated with your birthday (e.g., historical events that happened on your birthday, famous people who share your birthday, items such as your birthstone, etc.). Be sure to include the month and date of your birthday on your poster.

2. Art: Draw a picture of the birthday cake Molly sees in the bakery shop window (see p. 3 of the novel).

3. Writing/Drama: On a sheet of paper, describe a situation in which Emma tries to keep the peace between Molly and Elizabeth. (Suggestions: Emma insists that Molly walk with her and Elizabeth to the butcher shop. Emma says she will ask her mother for a similar cake on her birthday so both Elizabeth and Molly can taste it. Emma patiently explains American birthday customs to Molly.) What are the results? In groups of three, act out one of the above situations for the class.

4. Research: Research the Jewish celebration of Passover. Include historical information, food, games, rituals, and any other interesting facts about the holiday. Write three questions about Passover on separate note cards. Write the correct answer to each question on the back of the card. Give the note cards to your teacher. Your teacher will ask questions from the cards for the class to answer.

Make a Wish, Molly: Section Two, pp. 12–23

Mama makes Molly a sack lunch of acceptable foods to eat during Passover, but Molly hides it before she arrives at the party. Molly plans to eat cake and ice cream at Emma's party and not tell her mother. When the time comes, however, she simply cannot bring herself to do it. Elizabeth tells everyone that Molly will not eat the food because Jews will not eat in Christians' houses. Embarrassed, Molly excuses herself from the party and runs home.

Vocabulary
organdy
bodice
hedge
echoed
charades
streamers
encircled
brass
chandelier
crystal
applauded
laden
complicated
retorted

Discussion Questions

1. How does Molly plan to deal with the food served at Emma's party? *(Molly plans to eat the cake but not tell Mama.)*

2. What does Mama prepare for Molly to take to the party? What does Molly do with it? What are Mama's intentions? How does Molly feel about Mama's gesture? *(Mama fixes Molly a sack of foods that are acceptable to eat during Passover, including matzo and coconut macaroons. Molly throws the sack into a nearby hedge before she arrives at the party. Answers will vary. Suggestion: Mama intends to make things easier for Molly at the party by preparing a bag of food for her. Molly feels that bringing the bag of Jewish foods will be embarrassing and make her look different.)*

3. What clues does the author provide about the DeWitts' financial status? *(The DeWitts' house is in a nice neighborhood. The neighbor's house is a large, brick home with a hedge surrounding the front yard. Emma's house includes a dining room and luxury items such as a brass chandelier, a crystal bowl full of tulips, fine china plates and cups, and a large silver knife.)*

4. Does Molly eat the food that she is forbidden to eat during Passover? Why or why not? How does she explain her decision? *(No, she does not eat the cake. Answers will vary. Suggestion: She realizes that she cannot do something forbidden by her religious beliefs even though she wants to. She says she is not hungry.)*

5. What reason does Elizabeth give for Molly's decision? *(Elizabeth says that Jewish people will not eat in Christians' houses.)*

6. **Prediction:** What will happen to Molly and Emma's friendship?

Supplementary Activities

1. Characterization: Continue the Character Web for Molly (see p. 17 of this guide), and add any new information you have learned.

2. Art/Oral Presentation: On a sheet of paper, draw and cut out three large boxes to represent presents. Make a gift tag for each box. Label one tag "Molly," label another tag "Emma," and label a third tag "Elizabeth." On the back of each box, describe a gift you would like to give each character. Decorate the front side of each present. Share your ideas with the class, and explain why you chose each gift.

3. Social Studies: Research how people celebrate birthdays in another country. You may select any country you like besides the United States. Design a poster to present your research to the class. Be sure to include in your presentation the name and location of the country you selected.

Make a Wish, Molly: Section Three, pp. 24–36

Molly returns home, where Mama comforts her. At school, Emma and the other girls ignore Molly. Mama and Papa give Molly a gold heart necklace for Molly's birthday. Emma, Fay, and Elizabeth visit Molly's home to wish Molly a happy birthday. Emma gives Molly a birthday present, and Mama invites the girls in for rugelach. Molly's unplanned party is a success, and Molly learns that she isn't so different after all.

Vocabulary
miserable
discount
occasions
pinafore
hesitated
fashionably
prevent
outstretched
advance
Sabbath
flushed

Discussion Questions

1. What does Mama suggest to make Molly feel better? What does Molly think of Mama's idea? *(Mama suggests that Molly invite Emma and the other girls over for a party on Molly's birthday, which is soon approaching. Molly dismisses Mama's idea because she feels it would be embarrassing. She is afraid that Emma and the other girls would see that Molly's family and lifestyle are much different than their own.)*

2. Describe Molly and Emma's relationship at school after the party. *(Molly and Emma's relationship is strained. Molly apologizes for leaving the party, and Emma excuses Molly's outburst, but Molly no longer knows what to say to Emma. Molly avoids Emma and the other girls during recess. She and Emma speak to each other, but Molly doesn't feel like they are friends anymore.)*

3. What do Mama and Papa give Molly for her birthday? How does Molly respond? How does Emma respond? *(a gold heart necklace; Molly is excited and surprised and says, "Oh, Mama...oh, Papa, it's beautiful. It's so—so grown-up" [p. 27]. Emma notices Molly's necklace at school and says, "Oh, Molly, look at your necklace. It's so beautiful" [p. 28].)*

4. Who surprises Molly after school? Whose idea do you think it is to surprise Molly? Explain your answer. *(Emma, Fay, and Elizabeth surprise Molly by visiting Molly's home on her birthday. Answers will vary. Suggestions: It is probably Emma's idea to surprise Molly because Emma is a kind, thoughtful friend. Emma wishes Molly a happy birthday at school and later says, "When I went home for lunch, I told Mama we had to get you a present for your birthday" [p. 32].)*

5. Describe Molly's "unplanned" party. *(Mama brings out a large plate of rugelach and places a Sabbath candle in the center. The girls sing "Happy Birthday" to Molly. Molly makes a special birthday wish and blows out the candle.)*

6. How does Mama handle Elizabeth? *(Mama tells the girls, "After we eat off these plates and drink from these cups…Molly will carry them to the sink and I will wash them. We will all be able to eat from them again" [p. 34]. This proves that what Elizabeth said at Emma's party is untrue. Mama pokes Elizabeth in the shoulder when the other girls sing "Happy Birthday" so Elizabeth joins in.)*

7. For what does Molly wish? *(Molly wishes that she, Emma, and Fay will always be friends.)*

Supplementary Activities

1. Dialogue/Drawing Conclusions: Divide a sheet of paper into two columns. Title the page "Mama's Wisdom." Label the left column "About Being Different" and the right column "About Friends." Use the novels to find statements that reflect Mama's wisdom on each topic. Record each statement in the appropriate column. In the remaining space, explain why you think these statements are wise and how they apply to your life. (Answers will vary. Suggestions: About Being Different—"In one way or another we're all different" [p. 24]; "…in eleven days it's your birthday. We'll invite Emma and Fay and Elizabeth and the others here for a party. Then they'll see we're not so different" [p. 24]; "It's your birthday. That's a special occasion" [p. 28]. About Friends—"You don't have to plan a party in advance…. It's a party just because friends are together" [p. 34].)

2. Art: Draw Elizabeth, Fay, and Emma on a sheet of paper with a speech bubble over each character. In the speech bubbles, write how each character responds when Mama offers her rugelach. Beneath the drawings, explain what each character's response reveals about her. (Elizabeth—"We don't eat foreign foods" [p. 32]; Fay—"Is the wonderful smell in this house rugelach?… I eat rugelach" [p. 32]; Emma—"Me too" [p. 34]. Answers will vary. Suggestions: Elizabeth's response suggests that she is not open to trying new things from different cultures. Fay's response suggests that she is willing to try the rugelach because it smells delicious. Emma's response indicates that she is also willing to try the rugelach. Emma's and Fay's responses indicate that they have not prejudged the food just because it is from a different culture.)

Post-reading Discussion Questions

1. Why does Mama consider herself a Pilgrim? *(Molly tells Mama that Pilgrims are people who left their native countries in search of religious freedom in America. Molly's family came to America so they would no longer have to endure the oppression they experienced as Jewish people in Russia. Mama identifies with the Pilgrims because they came to the United States for the same reasons that she did.)*

2. Do you think Molly's situation will improve if Mama visits the school to speak with Miss Stickley? *(Answers will vary. Suggestions: Molly's situation might improve if Mama conferences with Molly's teacher. Miss Stickley might be more observant of how other students treat Molly and stop the teasing and insults. However, Molly's situation might not improve. If Mama visits Molly's school, other students might notice that Mama is different and make fun of Molly.)*

3. Do you think many other immigrant families live in Winter Hill? Why or why not? *(Answers will vary. Suggestions: No. Molly notes that there are no other Jewish children in her class. If there were immigrants from other countries, she most likely would have mentioned them. She probably wouldn't feel as alienated if there were other immigrant children with whom she could make friends.)*

4. What message do you think the author tries to send about the meaning of Thanksgiving? *(Answers will vary.)*

5. Why do you think Mama is so excited about Passover? Why isn't Molly excited? *(Mama is excited because the family will celebrate Passover for the first time in America, where they are free. Molly isn't as excited because she wants to taste ice cream and birthday cake at Emma's party, which Passover prohibits.)*

6. Compare and contrast Molly's and Emma's mothers. *(Answers will vary. Suggestions: Both Molly's and Emma's mothers are concerned and caring parents. They are kind to all people despite their differences, want the best for their daughters, and are willing to put forth extra effort to make things special for their daughters. Emma's mother is presumably American and owns expensive things such as fine china, a crystal bowl, and a brass chandelier. Molly's mother is a Russian Jewish immigrant and does not have expensive things but does a lot with the things she has.)*

7. Why does Elizabeth go to Molly's house with Emma and Fay? Is she right or wrong about Molly's home? *(Elizabeth wants to see if Molly's house is dirty and shabby. She is wrong.)*

8. Describe Mama's criteria for a good party. Do you agree? Why or why not? *(Answers will vary. Suggestion: According to Mama, a party is good because it involves friends and fun, not because of fancy decorations or expensive food. Answers will vary.)*

9. List some of Molly's assumptions about what people think of her. How does Molly learn that these assumptions are incorrect? *(Answers will vary. Suggestions: Molly thinks that people will not like her or Mama because they are Russian, Jewish, and poor. Molly learns that she is wrong when her friends visit her home on her birthday. Molly's "unplanned" party is such fun that it does not matter that Molly's family is not wealthy.)*

10. If you could change one part of either novel, what would you change? Why? *(Answers will vary.)*

Post-reading Extension Activities

1. Creative Thinking: Write the letters "A" to "Z" on a sheet of paper—one letter per line. Next to each letter, write at least one thing beginning with that letter for which you are thankful. (Example: A—apricots, B—Bubba, my dog, etc.). Remember to include things, people, feelings, ideas, places, etc.

2. Creative Thinking: Use the Attribute Web on page 20 of this guide to brainstorm ideas about the meaning of freedom.

3. Writing: Pretend you are Molly, and write a letter to Mama that explains at least three reasons why you are proud of her.

4. Social Studies/Oral Presentation: Research the period of American history from 1882 until 1924 to learn about immigration. From what countries did the immigrants travel? Where did they arrive? Where did they live, and what were the conditions like? Present your facts in a report to your class. Make a visual aid to include in your presentation.

5. Social Studies/Art: The First Amendment of the U.S. Constitution guarantees the following freedoms: religion, speech, press, assembly, and petition. Search newspapers and magazines to find examples of these freedoms and how they are used in modern society. Cut out articles and/or pictures to share with your class. Make a class collage of articles and photographs that exemplify freedom.

6. Research/Writing: Choose one of the following prominent Jewish figures: Albert Einstein, Jonas Salk, Levi Strauss, Irving Berlin, George and Ira Gershwin, Steven Spielberg, Emma Lazarus, or Ruth Handler. Research this person's life, including when and where he/she was born, where he/she grew up, why he/she is famous, and any other interesting facts about him/her. Write a biography of the person's life to share with the class. As a class, compile the biographies into a class book.

7. Research: Use the Internet and/or a local library to research immigration in the United States today. What are the four main reasons for legal immigration to America? How many people immigrate to the U.S. each year? From which countries do they travel? How does a person become a United States citizen? Summarize your findings in two paragraphs or less.

Assessment for *Molly's Pilgrim* and *Make a Wish, Molly*

Assessment is an ongoing process. The following eight items can be completed during study of the novels. Once finished, the student and teacher will check the work. Points may be added to indicate the level of understanding.

Name _____ Date _____

Student   **Teacher**

_____   _____   1. Complete a Story Map (see p. 21 of this guide) for either *Molly's Pilgrim* or *Make a Wish, Molly.*

_____   _____   2. List Elizabeth's negative comments about Molly, her family, and/or her culture. Use events from the stories to disprove Elizabeth's comments.

_____   _____   3. Complete the A Character's World activity on page 22 of this guide.

_____   _____   4. Write a two-paragraph book review of each novel to appear in your school newspaper. How many stars would you give each book? Why? Would you recommend this book to others? Why or why not?

_____   _____   5. Write four rules that explain how to treat someone from another culture. Base your rules on good and bad examples of how Molly is treated in the novels.

_____   _____   6. Complete the Thematic Analysis activity on page 23 of this guide.

_____   _____   7. List five words that communicate the most important ideas in *Molly's Pilgrim.* Make a second list of words for *Make a Wish, Molly.*

_____   _____   8. Use the following questions to evaluate the novels:

(a) Do you think *Molly's Pilgrim* is a good Thanksgiving story? Why or why not?
(b) Do you think *Make a Wish, Molly* is a good example of the dangers of stereotyping? Why or why not?
(c) What did you learn by reading these novels?
(d) In your opinion, what is each novel's main message?

Write your responses on a separate sheet of paper, and use complete sentences to answer each question. Support each response with facts and examples from the novels.

KWL

Directions: As the book or content area is studied, fill in this chart. Before reading, review what you KNOW about Judaism and the Jewish culture in the **K** column. The **W** column is for questions about these topics for which you WANT to find answers. The **L** column is completed after reading to list what you have LEARNED.

K	W	L

Getting the "Lay of the Land"

Directions: Prepare for reading by answering the following short-answer questions.

1. Who is the author?

   _____

2. What do the titles suggest to you about the novels?

   _____

   _____

   _____

   _____

3. When were the novels first copyrighted?

   _____

4. How many pages are there in each book?

   _____

5. Thumb through the novels. Read three pages from each novel—one from near the beginning, one from near the middle, and one from near the end. What predictions can you make about the novels?

   _____

   _____

   _____

   _____

   _____

6. What do the covers suggest to you about the novels?

   _____

   _____

   _____

   _____

   _____

   _____

Character Web

Directions: Complete the attribute web below by filling in information specific to Molly.

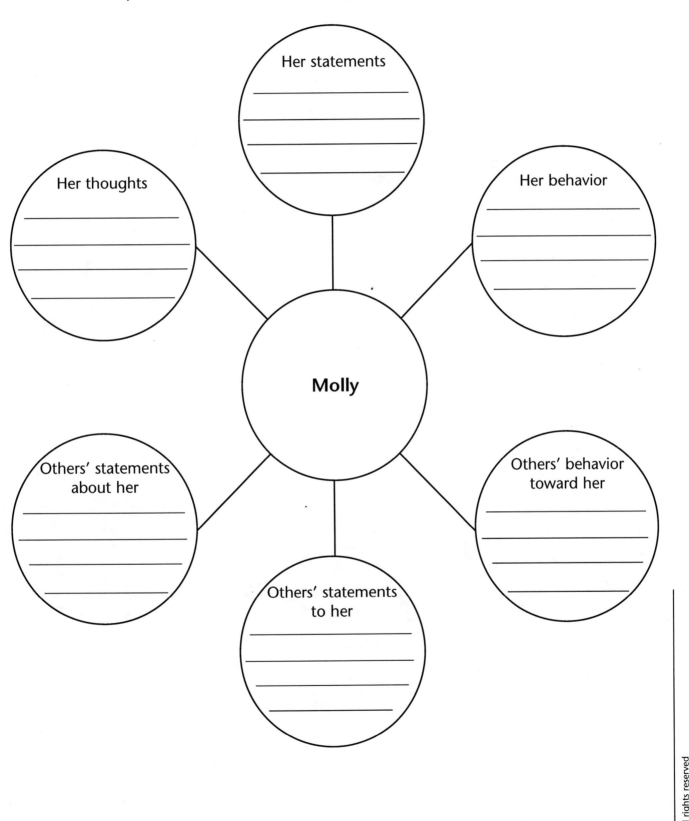

The Daily News

_____

_____

_____

_____

_____

_____

_____

_____

_____

_____

_____

_____

_____

_____

American Thanksgiving and the Feast of Tabernacles

Directions: Use the Venn diagram below to compare and contrast the Jewish Feast of Tabernacles and an American Thanksgiving.

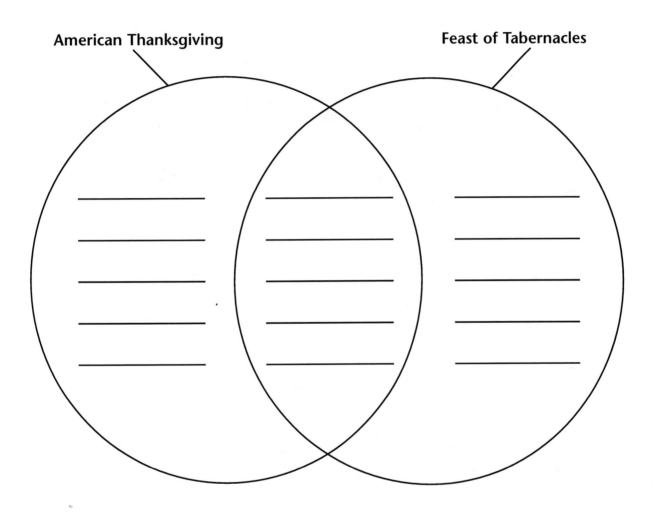

Attribute Web

Directions: Use the attribute web below to brainstorm ideas about the meaning of freedom.

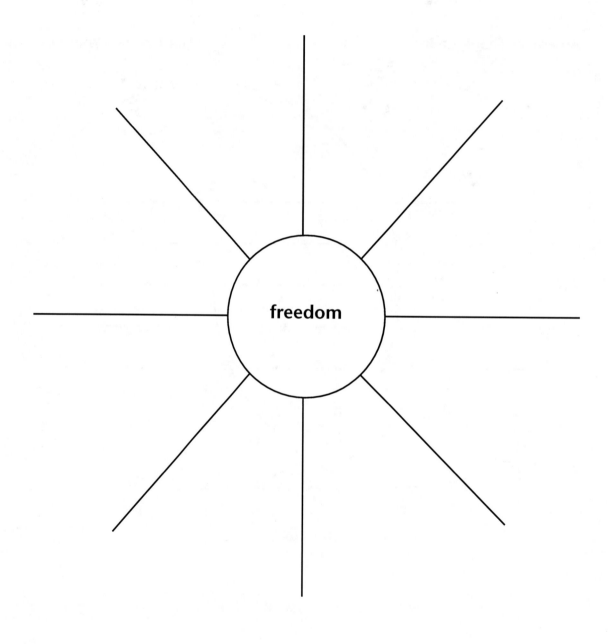

Story Map

Directions: Complete the story map for either *Molly's Pilgrim* or *Make a Wish, Molly*.

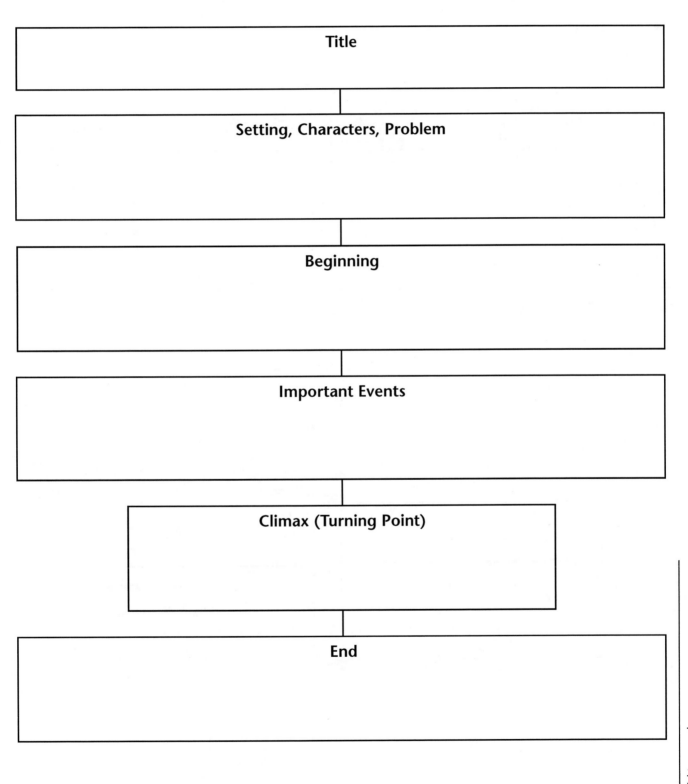

Title

Setting, Characters, Problem

Beginning

Important Events

Climax (Turning Point)

End

A Character's World

Directions: You may be able to draw parallels between a character's world and your own. Write a character's name in the blank. Describe that character's world. Then describe a related situation or event from your own world.

_____'s World

_____

_____

_____

My World

_____

_____

_____

_____'s World

_____

_____

_____

My World

_____

_____

_____

_____'s World

_____

_____

_____

My World

_____

_____

_____

_____'s World

_____

_____

_____

My World

_____

_____

_____

Thematic Analysis

Directions: Choose a theme from either book to be the focus of your word web. Complete the web, and then answer the question in each starred box.

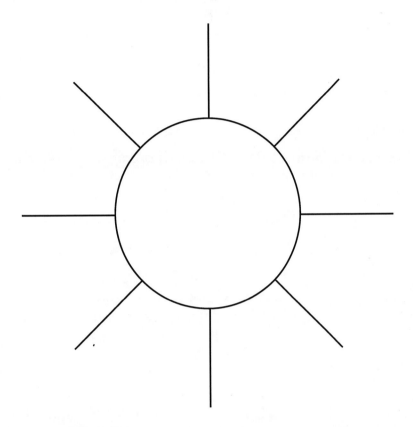

 What is the author's main message?

 What did you learn from the books?

Linking Novel Units® Lessons to National and State Reading Assessments

During the past several years, an increasing number of students have faced some form of state-mandated competency testing in reading. Many states now administer state-developed assessments to measure the skills and knowledge emphasized in their particular reading curriculum. The discussion questions and post-reading questions in this Novel Units® Teacher Guide make excellent open-ended comprehension questions and may be used throughout the daily lessons as practice activities. The rubric below provides important information for evaluating responses to open-ended comprehension questions. Teachers may also use scoring rubrics provided for their own state's competency test.

Please note: The Novel Units® Student Packet contains optional open-ended questions in a format similar to many national and state reading assessments.

Scoring Rubric for Open-Ended Items

3-Exemplary	Thorough, complete ideas/information Clear organization throughout Logical reasoning/conclusions Thorough understanding of reading task Accurate, complete response
2-Sufficient	Many relevant ideas/pieces of information Clear organization throughout most of response Minor problems in logical reasoning/conclusions General understanding of reading task Generally accurate and complete response
1-Partially Sufficient	Minimally relevant ideas/information Obvious gaps in organization Obvious problems in logical reasoning/conclusions Minimal understanding of reading task Inaccuracies/incomplete response
0-Insufficient	Irrelevant ideas/information No coherent organization Major problems in logical reasoning/conclusions Little or no understanding of reading task Generally inaccurate/incomplete response